A
JOYOUS
CHRISTMAS.
A wish of kindly meaning
and Greeting from a Friend.

001

002

To
wish you
Christmas Happiness.

003

A
MERRY
CHRISTMAS.
May all thy hours
be winged with Joy.

004

005

006

007

008

This Christmas bring Joy to your Heart.

009

Christmas in blessings of bright golden hours, to keep your heart as cheerful as the sweet sunny flowers.

010

A Merry Christmas

011

Fond Christmas Greetings

012

3

013

014

015

016

I hope
you'll have
a Merry
Christmas.

017

With best Christmas Wishes.

018

A
very Merry
Christmas
Dear.

019

020

021

May Christmas bring you loads of joy.

022

With Best Wishes

023

Christmas Greetings

024

A Merry Christmas to you.

025

: CHRISTMAS GREETINGS :

Good boys and girls upon this night
Are all in bed and sleeping tight;
For kids who watch have learned with cause
They never see kind Santa Claus.

026

027

A Merry Xmas

He's Looking for You

028

A MERRIE CHRISTMAS TO YOU.

"A merrie Christmas" to you! For we serve the Lord with mirth, And we carol forth glad tidings Of our holy Saviour's birth. So we keep the olden greeting With its meaning deep and true, And with "a merrie Christmas" And a happy New Year to you!

Frances Ridley Havergal.

029

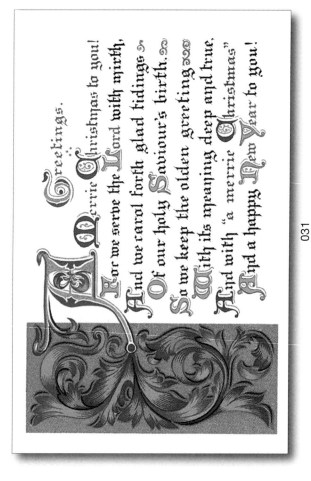

Greetings.

A Merrie Christmas to you!
For we serve the Lord with mirth,
And we carol forth glad tidings
Of our holy Saviour's birth.
So we keep the olden greeting
With its meaning deep and true,
And with "a merrie Christmas"
And a happy New Year to you!

031

Christmas Greetings.

033

A Joyful Yuletide

030

A Merry Christmas and Happy New Year

032

CHRISTMAS GREETINGS

035

CHRISTMAS WISHES

On this card
There is no room to say
What happy things
I wish for you
this joyous Yule-tide day.

037

A Joyful Christmas

034

Merry Christmas

036

9

038

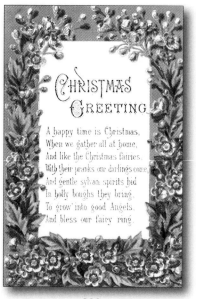

CHRISTMAS
GREETING

A happy time is Christmas,
When we gather all at home,
And like the Christmas fairies,
With their pranks our darlings come,
And gentle sylvan spirits bid
In holly boughs they bring,
To grow into good Angels,
And bless our fairy ring.

039

Think of me,
I'll
think of thee
At Christmas
tide.

040

A MERRY CHRISTMAS

A Christmas Greeting to you

041

043

042

CHRISTMAS GREETINGS

044

A Merry Christmas

045

Best Christmas Wishes

046

CHRISTMAS GREETINGS

047

11

Best Christmas Wishes

048

A Very Merry Christmas

049

MAY EVERY GOODLY GIFT COMBINE YOUR CHRISTMAS HOURS TO BLESS

CHRISTMAS GREETINGS

050

Christmas Greetings

051

052

053

054

055

13

056

057

058

059

060

061

062

063

064

15

A Merry CHRISTMAS

Joy attend
you,
Fortune send
you
Many Happy
Christmas Days.

065

A MERRY CHRISTMAS

066

Christmas Greetings.

067

You, dear, hang up your stockings all in a row
And see how fat Santa'll make 'em grow.

A Jolly Christmas

068

069

070

071

072

A MERRY CHRISTMAS.

073

Sing a song of Christmas,
    A bag of Christmas toys—
Santa Claus is bringing them
    To little girls and boys,
When the bag is opened,
    Won't the kiddies shout,
And then they'll play all
    Christmas Day,
And scatter things about.

074

075

076

*Loving Christmas Wishes.*

077

MERRY CHRISTMAS

A Very Happy Christmas to you all.
I hope you will like all the nice things
I left for you.   Good Bye.

078

Christmas Greetings

079

Christmas Greetings

080

081

A Joyful Christmas
to You

082

Many Happy
Returns
of the
DAY

083

084

A very merry CHRISTMAS!

085

086

087

088

089

YES WE'VE BEEN
VERY, VERY GOOD

090

A Merry Christmas.

091

MERRY
CHRISTMAS.

092

A Merry Christmas

093

094

095

096

097

098

May your **Christmas** be Happy

099

When Santa Claus
Next creeps
around,
Then wide awake
Shall I be
found.

For I want to
tell him
I'm tired of toys,
They're not much
good
To great big boys.

I'll ask
for a nice
little girl
full grown,
To be my
VERY, VERY
OWN

One who'll
ALWAYS
love me true,
In fact I want one
JUST LIKE
YOU

100

Christmas Greeting

101

102

103

105

104

106

108

110

107

109

112

114

111

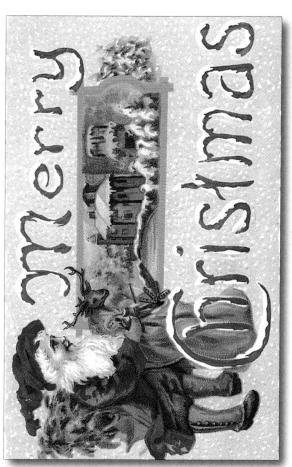

113

*Christmas Gladness*

To make some one happier with presents
Is the most joyful task of
Christmas.

115

*All Good Wishes for a Happy Christmas*

116

*A very Merry CHRISTMAS - - - - to you*

117

*Merry Christmas*

118

MERRY CHRISTMAS

119

120

A MERRY CHRISTMAS

121

122

123

124

125

A MERRY CHRISTMAS

126

127

128

129

130

131

132

133

134

135

Christmas
Greetings

136

137

138

May all the
Christmas Joys
be Yours

139

33

140

141

142

143

CHRISTMAS GREETING.

A Happy Christmas to you, dearest friends,
We think of you to-day with memories dear,
As in the darkness, flowers out of sight,
Still whisper with their fragrance to the night,
"Forget us not, unseen we yet are near."

144

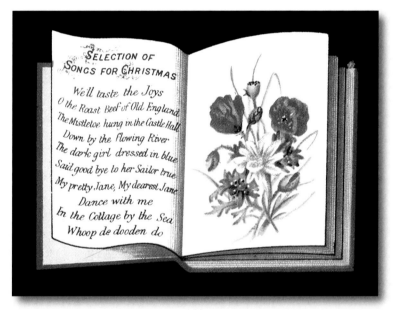

SELECTION OF
SONGS FOR CHRISTMAS

We'll taste the Joys
O the Roast Beef of Old England
The Mistletoe hung in the Castle Hall
Down by the flowing River
The dark girl dressed in blue
Said good bye to her Sailor true
My pretty Jane, My dearest Jane
Dance with me
In the Cottage by the Sea
Whoop de dooden do

146

147

A Christmas Wish.

At Christmas,
be merry and thank God for all!
And feast thy poor neighbours
The great and the small.

145

PEACE BE TO THEE

Behold I bring you tidings of great joy which shall be to all people.

148

35

Christmas Greetings

149

A MERRY CHRISTMAS TO YOU

150

A MERRY CHRISTMAS

151

A Happy CHRISTMAS to You

152

153

154

155

156

WISHING YOU CHRISTMAS CHEER

All Good Wishes send I thee, Merry may your Christmas be.

157

A Merry Christmas.

158

A merry Christmas

159

WISHING YOU CHRISTMAS CHEER

A simple wish, A greeting true, A hope that Santa's good to you.

160

161

Wishes come and wishes go
Every Christmas time 'tis so,
None more tender, none more true,
Than this wish of mine to you.

162

163

164

165

166

167

168

169

All Good Wishes for Christmas.

170

A jolly time this Christmas

171

Wishing you a Merry Christmas

172

Merry Christmas

173

MAY SANTA FILL YOUR STOCKING FULL.

174

A LOAD OF GOOD WISHES
FOR A MERRY CHRISTMAS

175

A MERRY Christmas

176

A Merry Christmas

177

179

181

178

180

182

183

184

185

186

187

188

189

190

Here comes a big
hearty wish for a
Merry Christmas.

191

Sweetheart Days

A Merry Xmas

192

A MERRY CHRISTMAS

193

A MERRY CHRISTMAS

Here's a fine fellow, as gay as can be,
For all of his presents just fit to a T.

194

195

196

197

198

A Happy Christmas

**HAWTHORN.**

CHRISTMAS WISH.

Pilgrim to a better land,
Here behold a waymark stand!
Be thy pathway full of peace,
Strewn with joys that never cease,
And with virtue shining bright
To the perfect day of light.

CHARLOTTE M YONGE.

199

200

A Merry Christmas to you.

201

202

CHRISTMAS WISHES.

Blessings attend you
Wherever you go,
Pleasure and plenty,
And peace,
Far from your path
Be all trouble and woe,
May your happiness
Grow and increase.

203

A MERRY CHRISTMAS bright and gay.

204